The waves beside them danced; but they
Out-did the sparkling waves in glee:
A poet could not but be gay,
In such a jocund company.

WILLIAM WORDSWORTH

The
Wildflower

Bette Woolsey Castro

National Wildflower Research Center

Introduction by
LADY BIRD JOHNSON

Foreword by
HELEN HAYES

Starwood Publishing, Inc.
Washington, D.C.

Illustrated by Marjorie Stodgell
Designed by Adrianne Onderdonk Dudden
Poems copyright © 1991 by Bette Woolsey Castro.
All rights reserved.
Copyright © 1991 by Starwood Publishing, Inc.
All rights reserved.
No part of the contents of this book
may be reproduced without the
written permission of the publisher.
ISBN 0-912347-79-1
Printed in Singapore by Tien Wah Press
5 4 3 2 1   98 97 96 95 94 93 92 91

For Nash,
Kim, and Kristen
with love

Contents

The trumpet creeper and the hummingbird

The day lily

Queen Anne's lace

Lady's-slippers at Dragon Rock

Indian paintbrush

Wildflowers of the Tetons

Roadside wildflowers

Black-eyed Susans on the parkway

Wild rose, white butterfly

Midsummer in the garden

Daisy

Wildflowers of Martha's Vineyard

Wildflowers of Hawaii

Goldenrod

Indian blanket

A symphony of coreopsis

The wood aster

Foreword

When I was very young, I liked to creep off to a field near my grand-mother's farm in Maryland, find a patch of wildflowers—red clover or field daisies or such—curl up in it, and dream beautiful dreams. I did not realize how important these spells of perfumed privacy were to me till life stepped up and took them away. I have been missing them for years, but no more; fate has repented and given them back.

Bette Castro has made it possible for me to have spring on the coldest, darkest winter days and wildflowers all year long. All I have to do is sit by an open fire, book in hand, and soon my memory will collaborate with the lovely words on the page, and I will be transported to where the violets grow in May. *The Wildflower* is a blessed book.

Helen Hayes
Co-Chairman
National Wildflower Research Center

Introduction

This delightful collection has been drawn from the author's close acquaintance with, respect for, and love of that miraculous gift of nature, the bounteous family of native plants which grace our nation. For anyone who finds special magic in the music of both wildflowers and poetry, Bette Castro's words speak to the heart. She has captured the essence of wildflowers, giving us a heightened sense of community with the natural world.

An astute observer once wrote, "The world is so great and rich, and life so full of variety that you can never lack occasions for poems." Thus it is for Bette Castro. I hope you will savor, as I have, a joyful affinity with her discoveries and the sensitive voice she brings to them.

Lady Bird Johnson
Co-Chairman
National Wildflower Research Center

Preface

This book springs from my lifelong love of poetry and wildflowers and from my continuing delight in the many ways they nourish the soul. Inspired by the founding of the National Wildflower Research Center in 1982 by Lady Bird Johnson, and encouraged by the Founding President, Nash Castro, and Co-Chairman, Helen Hayes, I began this poetic journey.

Few issues are more critical than restoring the natural biological diversity of our land, and the National Wildflower Research Center is dedicated to that end. All royalties from the sale of this book will be donated to the center so that it may continue its fine work.

It is my hope that *The Wildflower* will bring to others an added appreciation of the priceless heritage wildflowers represent and further their use in our landscapes, for our enjoyment and that of future generations.

Bette Woolsey Castro

Wildflowers

They grow in random, scattered splendor,
A magical blending of the land's bright hues,
Stretching across the hills and valleys
In never-ending majesty.

We call these magic flowers wild—
Wild because they scorn man's power
And live and thrive without his care,
Wild because through drought and storm
They ride the winds to bring the seasons
That lift the heart.

A glorious tapestry,
God's own needlepoint!
Forever brilliant,
Forever wondrous,
Forever wild!

An azalea walk in May

Wild azaleas, mossy rocks,
Cinquefoil of palest gold,
Violets, and wintergreen,
And buttercups unfold.

Shades of green with sunlight bright,
Leaves shimmer in the wind.
Nature's ever-wondrous spring
Comes to life again.

As part of nature's greater plan,
The birds join in the plea:
Revere, conserve, protect our land
For all who come to see.

Man tries and often will surmise
His efforts are in vain,
But in the beauty of the land
The spring will come again!

Spring conference amid the dogwood

A conference of natural beauty—
Umbrellas of dogwood
Shading groups of bluebells
Conferring with pale blue phlox
And violets white;
Trilliums nodding their assent
To join the iris
In their sublime production of beauty.

Planning takeovers of woodland paths,
An all-out assault on the senses of man;
Bringing him to bargain
For the priceless beauty of spring.

Common dandelion

Odes to roses, odes to lilies,
And the thousand daffodils
Yet no bard describes your splendor,
And no song salutes you still.

Heedless of your worth and beauty,
One by one you are maligned.
Banished from the tended landscape,
Golden exiles are your kind.

Yet in childhood's purest wonder,
Heart-dreamt wishes were your ken.
Silken down released your magic:
Blow and blow again!

Ever striving, ever constant,
Spring's new hope you do define.
Sturdy flower of unsung valor,
Grow and thrive—
Your song is mine!

Desert wildflowers in springtime

They spread their joy 'neath desert skies,
Too glorious for the artist's skills,
Surrounded by majestic peaks,
The celebrated rocks and rills.

They speak of time, of eons past,
Of dinosaur and reptile rare.
They speak of man's relentless quest,
Undaunted, fearless pioneers.

Harsh nature tries their souls' own strength.
Survive, endure with hardships great,
Thirst, fade, retreat, their beauty gone,
And then revive to bloom again.

Each prickled cactus wears a bud,
Each spiny shoot a leaf,
The giant wears its Easter crown
Of blossoms white and sweet.

As if in her imperial way
Nature does so decree
That every thorny desert plant
Share in her great glory.

Violets

When early spring puts on her coat
The season to foretell,
You come in purple splendor
To grace her wide lapel.

Spring beauty

God's synonym for spring is beauty:
Beauty in the woodland paths,
Beauty in the sky's soft azure,
Beauty in the green of grass.

Beauty in the leaves so verdant,
Beauty in the birds' sweet call,
Beauty in the flower patterns
That embroider nature's mall.

From the earth's deep winter harshness
Blooms a dainty, pink-hued throng.
Drifts of joy again surround us.
The spring beauty comes along.

Trillium

Splendid flower of purest white,
Shining in rich woodlands green,
Sentinels of gleaming light
In the paths unseen.

Were you designed in pristine splendor
With a mission still obscure?
Or will your gift to man be measured
By your grace and beauty pure?

Splendid trillium, graceful flower,
Raise your petals to the sun.
Let us know that where there's beauty
Art and life become as one.

The trout lily

Fragile as a fairy's wings,
Elfin flower of mottled yellow,
Making woodpaths bright with sun
And the senses mellow.

Tiny drops of gold bestrewn
In the meadow's glen,
Telling nature's tale of spring
O'er and o'er again!

A wildflower sampler

A wildflower sampler on the wall,
Fashioned by a daughter's hand,
Colored with love and time and care,
Outlining forms of flowers fair.

An anemone begins the lot,
Favorite of all artists bold,
Sepals of red and purple hue,
Royal robes were inspired by you.

Next along the bud-strewn path
Of blossoms, leaves, and vines
Come the fireweed, rose, and phlox
And the lovely columbine.

A bee sits lightly on a bud
Stitched with a thread so fine,
Sipping nectar from its cup,
The quest of his lifetime.

A sampler on the wall of life
Fashioned, too, with love and care,
Threads of wonder and of joy,
Weaving dreams in patterns rare.

O dual samplers of bold design,
Hark to a dreamer's plea:
Let not the cares of time bedim
What you were meant to be.

When winter's cold and the wheel of life
Have worn your colors thin,
When memory's ghost and nature's hand
Know not where to begin,

Hold to the magic, hold to the dream,
Let not your pattern wane.
Hope and faith and love will come
To weave you o'er again!

Buttercup

A cup to hold the morning dew,
Butter yellow in your hue,
You brighten all of nature's way.
Buttercup, be here to stay.

Bestow your joy in grass and field,
Make somber clouds and shadows yield.
Buttercup, be here to stay.
Brighten every living day.

Bluebonnet

Spreading beauty near and far,
Lupine flower of blue,
Filling roadsides, meadows, fields,
With a sea of brightest hue.

A golden hill of coreopsis
Joins you in your lavish show.
Daisies, phlox, and blushing primrose
Spread their joy for all to know.

You stand out in cobalt splendor,
A painting by the Lord's own hand,
Nature's brush dipped in His medium,
Lavished over our fair land.

Touching minds and hearts and senses
With your wild, tumultuous scene,
You indeed are nature's sonnet.
Hail to you, O bright bluebonnet!

A poppy field at play

I paused in life's demanding role
Beside a meadow green,
And all at once I felt a spell
Of merriment most keen.

The poppies there in festive garb
Smiled bright as if at play,
Beckoning me to stop and dream
Ere I went on my way.

The inner self of industry
Debated with the soul.
To sow, to weed, to reap we must
Before our hopes grow old.

My heart received the message
From the blooms along life's way,
From wildflowers gaily planted
To seam the night and day.

When elusive time besets me
And life's pace begins to weigh,
In memory I then return
To the poppy field at play.

The trumpet creeper
and the hummingbird

I watched from my window
As the hummingbird came,
Swift as lightning,
His wings a song in motion.

Dipping into the brilliant blossom,
His slender beak
Took the nectar once again
As man takes the beauty of the flower
To renew the joy of living.

The day lily

Short is your life like man's
Yet filled with grace and beauty.
Yours is a season of warmth and joy,
Languid soft winds that move the spirit,
Warm rain refreshing all that is green.

Summer in the stream of life,
You awaken with the morn's rebirth,
And in the twilight's ever-growing shadow
You close your eyes and dream.

Queen Anne's lace

Showy plant of lacy beauty
Fit for any queen,
Decorating highway roadsides
And lush meadows green.

Did the fairies spin your pattern,
Embroidering nature's land for all?
Do they pause beneath your shelter
When the rains begin to fall?

Did the fairy princess choose you
For her coronation gown?
Does she wear you still in splendor
As her nation's queen renowned?

No royal ermine is your equal,
No treasured lace supreme.
You capture summer's light and beauty,
Spread grace where'er you're seen.

Fit for a queen indeed, I sigh.
I only wish the queen were I!

Lady's-slippers
at Dragon Rock

Carved into a dragon rock,
A crystal pond of blue,
Harsh with granite's somber glare,
No vestige of beauty there

Till on its banks in paths unseen
The fairy elves arrive,
Fashioning lady's-slippers fair.
Beauty then is everywhere.

Texture of moonbeams,
Colors sublime,
Each lady's-slipper
Is beauty's own rhyme.

Indian paintbrush

Ragged plant whose vermillion bracts
Transform the desert drab,
You gather reflections of the sun,
Turning them to red-orange pigments,
Tinged with nature's gold.

Dipping your leaves into their magic,
You paint the secrets of our landscape
With glowing, scarlet fervor,
Dazzling the beholder,
Enriching his senses
With the lasting gift of beauty.

Wildflowers of the Tetons

The misty dawn obscures the peaks.
Their image faint belies
The splendor that is soon to come
Into the great wide skies.

The utter grandeur of God's works,
The glorious majesty,
Are quiet now in gray repose,
Their wonders yet to be.

And then the sun whose yellow whip
The muse has long portrayed
Comes out across the grassy plains
To drive the mist away.

The sagebrush all in garb of gray
Now takes a rosy hue.
Fireweed, foxtail, and fairy bells
Dispel the morning dew.

The alpine daisy tries once more
To match the sun with gold,
And flaming Indian paintbrushes
Their petaled wheels unfold.

The laggard sun again becomes
The master of the day
And all of nature's magic meld
Quite takes the breath away!

Roadside wildflowers

Nature's busy fingers
Far into the curtained night
Embroider wildflower motifs
For man's pure delight,

Using as her palette
Colors of sun and sky,
Bedazzling with her vivid hues
The awestruck passerby.

Life's bouquet unfolding,
Harbinger of change and time,
Entangles plants and flowers
With man's ever-living rhyme.

Wildflowers of the roadside,
Give to us the clue.
Assault us with your colors,
Let us your strength imbue.

Share your verve and beauty,
Release the soul from strife.
Teach us to forever heed
The poetry of life.

Black-eyed Susans on the parkway

A parkway edges a mighty river,
Threading the land harmoniously.
Wildflowers along a green-ribbon oasis
Lead from the city of steel,
Carrying men to and from
The dailiness of life.

Black-eyed Susans gaily cluster,
Flashing their kohl-rimmed eyes,
Rehearsing their collective roles,
Presenting in pell-mell order
A coherent vision of joy,
Promising gentle respite
From the day's labors,
Allowing the tender power of flowers
To ease the journey home.

Wild rose, white butterfly

Silken petals, silken wings
A flutter of white;
Poignant, playful closeness.

Unexpected moments
Of the heart's recall.
Distant memories of joy
And happiness shared.

Miraculous matter
Within your gossamer wings;
Is the mystery of your message
The sweet foreverness of love?

Midsummer in the garden

Shafts of sunlight filtering through,
Paling the leaves of green,
Brighten the morn's crisp awakening.
Bird song in dulcet tones
Colors the air with a message of hope.

The garden languishes in midsummer
   stillness.
Gone are the periwinkle, violet, and daffodil.
The day lily has turned to green-leaf slumber
And the wild geranium now commands
   the eye.

But oh, the rose!
How splendidly it rallies
To bloom again in soft, glorious abandon,
Giving its notice to all
That summer still demands to live!

Daisy

Wildflower brave, oh speak to me
Of nature's own fidelity.
Speak of endurance, strength, and grace,
And of the world's victorious pace.

Speak of joys, of transient woes,
Life's treasured dreams that come and go,
And of continuous liberty
From harsh constraints that need not be.

Daisy, poppy, aster blue,
Let man aspire to be like you,
Showing your colors for all to see
Your heavenly tryst with destiny.

Wildflowers of Martha's Vineyard

Morning seeps in, shrouding the island
   in mist.
Remnants of yesteryear's vineyards
Outline lanes to today's hideaways.
Man's search for solitude and respite
Finds fulfillment in the early dawn.

Wildflowers nodding to fellow wild grasses
Converse in their mysterious ways,
Hostage to man's need for escape
Yet ever mindful of the lives they touch
With beauty and with joy.

Summer mariners man their vessels
To test the soft sea's swells,
And all who gaze in peaceful contemplation
Find solace in the tender power
Of the Vineyard's wildflowers.

Wildflowers of Hawaii

The winds of heaven blew,
Covering an island with blossoms—
Orchids, plumeria, pikake
For the goddess Pele.

Winds stirred the ohias,
Filling the air
With island perfume,
Carrying bird song
In tones of tropic life,

Telling of ancient rhythms and customs,
The melding of old and new:
Ginger so white,
Speaking of love and virtue,
Ginger so red,
Speaking of fire and stress.

O blossoms of the islands,
Let your magic spread
To touch the heart of man!

Goldenrod

As summer sheds her posied gown
To put on autumn's dress,
You stand in radiant golden garb
Along the roadside's crests.

The languid air hangs heavily
In the warmth of yellow sun,
And the scent of woodland asters
Says that autumn has begun.

The sumac shows its scarlet leaf
Your tasseled head below,
And the thistle's browning, spiny burr
Adds texture to the show.

When rampant heat and rocky soil
Discourage seed and pod,
None spreads its wealth more freely
Than the splendid goldenrod.

Indian blanket

Colors of earth and fire and sun
Across the prairie dry
Recall bright tribal wheels of fire,
Rites danced 'neath a burning sky.

A work of glory in texture and form,
A vibrant and valiant flower
Graces the land with myths beyond time,
Bringing the desert to fervent rhyme.

A symphony of coreopsis

A composition of ardent chords
Played along the blue highways of the land,
Singing the passion of all things free,
Coloring the tide stream of life
In hues of glorious yellow.

Fresh generations of your kin
Will write earth's secret melody:
Visions of full-flowering wonder,
Infinite notes of beauty
To lift the hopes of man.

The wood aster

Aster splendid, aster blue,
So widespread is your face,
Another time, another world
Did you the landscape grace?

Did horses' hooves transport you
Across the fertile land?
Did tender winds direct you
Into crevices and sand?

Did your love affair with nature
Exact from her a pledge
Bequeathing you a special role
Along the roadside's edge?

Do you slumber in quiescence
Till autumn her poem writes,
Using you as grace notes
To her gold-red songs of life?